40 DAYS &
40 NIGHTS

Manifestation Key

40 DAYS & 40 NIGHTS

JOHN & EMILY

Eternally Grateful

4 Your Love

Always

+1

ALSO BY EILEEN COLTS:

Mandela Effect: Friend or Foe?

40 DAYS
&
40 NIGHTS

Manifestation Key

Eileen Colts

The author and the publisher of this book do not dispense medical advice or prescribe the use of any technique as treatment for medical, physical, mental, or emotional problems without the advice of a physician.

The intent of this book is to offer information and opinion only. In the event you use any of the information in this book for yourself, the author and the publisher assume no liability or responsibility for your actions.

11:11 Publishing House, LLC
20791 Three Oaks Parkway, Unit 809
Estero, Florida 33929 USA
ISBN: 9781672048552

Contents

CHAPTER 1
The Mystical Number 40

The number forty (spelled fourty until the seventeenth century), like all numbers, has special significance in Numerology, where the sacred aspects of numbers are used to predict life-changing events, fortuitous times, personality traits and one's life mission or destiny.

The number 40 is equivalent to the properties of the number 4: $40 = 4 + 0 = 4$ which is numerologically the number for life planning, organization, and dependability; for creating, implementing, executing and expanding something lasting or important; encompassing the whole; all details, the big picture; implementing projects; the take action number in business, relationships, life; hard but worthwhile work; taking stock, important adjustments, affecting the whole, startling growth, and worldwide effects.

Number 4 traits are strong and loyal, grounded, and 'down to Earth'. Four is the number for building foundations, buildings, and doorways. Four is common sense, to make firm, and to strengthen. The number four provides the foundation for many **Earth cycles**: the **four seasons** of Spring, Summer, Autumn, and Winter; the four phases or quarters of the **Moon**; the **Four elements** Air, Water, Earth and Fire; and the **four cardinal directions** North, South, East and West. All of these form the building blocks of matter in the here-now, and are the very essence of form in the quantum world. No wonder the number 40, which always reduces to 4 in numerology, is so significant.

In terms of **Destiny** in numerology, depending on the source, the number 40 symbolically represents the waiting, the preparation, the test, and the achievement of reaching for salvation, atonement, enlightenment, Heaven, Nirvana, Shambhala – in other words one's highest possible state of being in the current lifebody. This could be interpreted as a kind of symbolic death of the ego and a spiritual rebirth.

The mysterious and ancient **Four Pillars** refer to an ancient **Chinese** fortune telling system called the

Four Pillars of Destiny. You may think there are only two pillars in the politically and financially powerful not-so-secret society of **Freemasonry**, but some of their buildings actually have Four Pillars - maybe because they trace their roots all the way back to **Ancient Egypt**. There are Four Pillars of Heaven in the Egyptian hieroglyph tjs-ut. The Four World Pillars in Ancient Egyptian mythology that held up the heavens also represented the four cardinal points of North, South, East and West. The famous Pyramids of Giza have four sides (and a base) not three.

More modern references include: Four Pillars of Nepal Bhasa, representing the four people who spearheaded a campaign to revive the language and literature. Four Pillars of Transnistria, which is the declaration of independence of a separatist region in Moldova in Eastern Europe. Four pillars of policy of the Australian government to maintain the separation of the four largest banks. *Four Pillars,* a research program from the Geneva Association. Four Pillars of Dominican Life which represent the principles of the Dominican Order. Four Pillars of manufacturing and engineering devised by the American SME association supporting manufacturing. The Four Pillars of Green Politics: ecological wisdom, social justice, grassroots democracy and non-violence. The Four Pillars of the 1990s All Japan Pro Wrestling.

The significance of the number 40 extends well

beyond mysticism and pillars, representing iconic life phrases and phases. An average human pregnancy is 40 weeks; 40 below is the only temperature the same in Celsius and Fahrenheit; Venus forms a pentagram in the sky every eight years returning to its original point every 40 years and has a 40 day regression period of moving in the opposite direction; in the British Grand National horse race the maximum number of entrants is 40; for many, 'life begins at forty'; some like 'catching 40 winks'; Western cultures usually have a standard 40-hour work week; freed slaves in America were offered 40 acres and a mule; maritime quarantine is 40 days since the Bubonic Plague; Ali Baba had forty thieves; an Arabic Proverb states: "to understand a people you must live among them for 40 days"; Russian folklore says spirits linger for 40 days at the place of their death; historically 40 lashes with a whip was a standard punishment; popular songs were listed in the American Top 40; there are 40 rods in a furlong; 40 yards in a bolt of fabric; a rainbow can only be seen in the morning or late afternoon, because it only occurs when the Sun is up to (rising) or below (setting) 40 degrees above the horizon!

Conclusion: 40 is a powerful number for among other things, manifestation, growth, and change, but it really shines forth in all its glory in the Abrahamic religions of the ancient Middle East, and the Near East.

CHAPTER 2

The Sacred Number 40

In the **Hebrew Bible**, which also became the **Old Testament**, forty is often used to separate epochs. For instance, the Israelites wandered outside of the Promised Lands for forty years – meaning "for a generation". Abraham asked God not to destroy Sodom and Gomorrah if he could find 40 righteous people living there. When Jacob died in Egypt, they embalmed his body for 40 days. During the Great Flood it rained for forty days and forty nights. Noah waited for forty nights after first seeing mountain tops to release a bird to confirm nearby land. Moses spent forty days and forty nights on Mount Sinai three times. He sent out reconnaissance teams to explore the Promised Land of Canaan for forty days. Goliath challenged the Israelites for forty days before David slew him. Elijah walked for forty days and nights to Mount Horeb. Jonah warned the ancient city of Nineveh of its destruction for 40 days. Moses lived in Egypt and the desert for 40 years each before leading his people out of slavery. The Book of Exodus has 40 chapters. Before King Saul, the Holy Land was ruled by Judges who served 40-year-terms. Many Jewish Kings ruled for forty years (a generation) including Saul, David and Solomon. A man must reach his 40th year before he may study Kabbalah. Water was measured in units of 40 (a mikvah). In Hebrew **Gematria,** the number 40 is a value also attributed to the words: life, I am, aim, am I, and kali (as in Kali Yuga – the Hindu period of sleeping consciousness we are now reportedly leaving). This is not the only connection between Hebrew and Hindu. In Hebrew, shiva means seven and relates to the Jewish seven-day mourning period (within a larger period of mourning) for the immediate family of a deceased loved one. In Hindu Shiva is known as "The Destroyer" and "The Creator" within the Trimurti, the Hindu trinity including Brahma and Vishnu. In Shaivism, Shiva is one of the supreme beings who creates, protects and transforms the universe through destruction and rebirth, much like the mythical phoenix. Some even believe the New Testament is a Near-Eastern correction of the Old Testament, after Jesus went missing for decades according to some, studying Near Eastern Mysticism where the Three Magi (Three Kings of Orient) hailed from.

Much of the Old Testament was based on ancient **Mesopotamian**, **Sumerian**, **Babylonian** myths found in cuneiform clay tablets in modern day Iraq. These tablets, many of which may be read on an Oxford University online library (1) are considered to be the oldest forms of human writing ever found, dating back at least five thousand years. That does not mean they will remain so, as excavations of older temples like Gobekli Tepe in Turkey, some twelve thousand years old, have not been completed. In fact, Zecharia Sitchin (2) made the Annunaki and their approaching rogue planet Nibiru popular from these same tablets. Sound far-fetched? NASA recently confirmed a mysterious super-sized planet is likely out past Neptune (tilting our Solar System), which they call the new Planet 9 just ten years after Pluto was dethroned of that title. (3)

An earlier version of Noah and the Great Flood is found in the Babylonian Epic Poem of Gilgamesh in the Sumerian clay tablets; along with the earlier Biblical Genesis stories with Adam, his first wife Lilith who left him (becoming a demon-goddess in the process), and his second wife Eve representing the first humans.

In these religious myths that inspired the

Abrahamic religions like Judaism, Christianity, and Islam, the god of intelligence, crafts, creation and water is Enki (aka Ea) - who had the sacred number 40. The Israelites spent so much time in this region of Canaan some consider them one of the Canaanite tribes. So it is no surprise they absorbed earlier religious traditions from the area (much like Christianity later absorbed pagan dates and practices from the areas it invaded).

In **Christianity** 40 was also used to mean "a long time". This may have been due to shorter human lifespans. During the Temptation of Christ, Jesus fasted for 40 days and 40 nights in the desert. Forty days is the exact period of days between the Resurrection and the Ascension. Before his crucifixion, Jesus predicted the destruction of Jerusalem, which occurred 40 years after his death. Lent, a repentance and denial period in preparation for Easter, lasts 40 days. The earliest Christian martyrs of Sebaste, who were put to death in modern day Turkey in 320 A.D. numbered 40.

In ancient **Catholic** practice, the dead are commemorated for 40 days from their death when the immediate family wear only black. A mass and a small feast are held during the 40-day period, and the 40th day is considered the deceased relative's judgment day. The mourning period for **Eastern Orthodox Christians** also lasts for 40 days, but for close relatives, the mourning period may last a year, during which only black clothing is worn.

Traditionally, the **Muslim** mourning period also lasts 40 days. Depending on the degree of religiousness of the family, widows are expected to observe a longer mourning period of four months and ten days.

In **Islam** around 600 A. D., Muhammad was 40 years old when he began receiving revelation in a cave from Archangel Gabriel (from the Old Testament/New Testament stories and Sumerian myths). He fasted for 40 days before receiving revelation and he began Islam with only 40 followers.

In his inspired verbal teachings, which were written down becoming the **Quran (Koran)**, God forbade non-believers from entering the Holy Land for 40 years. In the Quran Muhammad retells the story of Moses receiving the Ten Commandments on Mount Sinai after 40 days and 40 nights there. The Prophet Isa was tempted in the desert by Satan for 40 days. Masih as-Dajjal, the equivalent of the anti-Christ, roamed the Earth for 40 days and nights. And two prophets after Muhammad, Dawuud and Suleiman, each ruled for 40 years.

There are 40 paragraphs in the last day of **Sikh** prayers called Anand Sahib.

One Mandala Kalam in **Hinduism** is a period of 40 days of fasting. The **Sindhi Hindu** community observe the festival Chaliha Sahib in thanks to God for 40 days.

In **Buddhism,** there are 40 Meditation Subjects

considered challenging instructional topics on which to meditate and contemplate for personal enlightenment. There are four types of Buddhism: Traditional (modern) Buddhism, Nikaya Buddhism, Mahayana (which includes Zen Buddhism), and Vajrayana Buddhism (which has four further schools).

The Buddha taught there were four types of friends: the Helper, the Enduring Friend, the Mentor, and the Compassionate Friend. The four stages of enlightenment in early Buddhism are Sotāpanna, Sakadāgāmi, Anāgāmi, and Arahant, with four Noble Truths on the Eight Fold Path. There are also four stages of reincarnation, or Bardos, in the cycle of rebirth. The natural bardo of your current life, the bardo of dying, the bardo of dharmata (which lasts from the moment of death and continues until visions of perfection are complete), and the karmic bardo of becoming (which continues until a new rebirth is made in physical form again).

The pre-Buddhist 4 Brahma Viharas, or The Four Divine Virtues of Buddhism of Metta are: Loving Kindness, Compassion, Sympathetic Joy, and Equanimity. They are considered key meditative practices that heal and enlighten not only the person, but their community, the world and the universe.

What are the 4 main principles of **Confucianism**? After 500 B.C. Confucius, (meaning Master Kong), taught 4 religious concepts that became a popular life philosophy many consider a religion. The four pillars of Confucianism are generally considered to be: respect, righteousness, reverence, and justice. These represent the moral principles identified in Confucian Ethics to transform a society, starting with the individual, into a successful sacred whole.

CHAPTER 3
How I Found 40 Days & 40 Nights

After my Near Death Experience (NDE) at the age of 17 while living with my Father, Tom, in Egypt, (see About the Author), I began searching for the meaning of life and the nature of God in earnest. This led me to exploring world religions and quantum science for the next 40+ years (I have yet to stop). I took this quest into a Jesuit University, but I could only adequately study the *Bible* in that setting, so the world of the *Quran*, *Kabbalah*, *Mahabharata*, the *Sutras*, et cetera came later. Along with metaphysical classics like *A Course in Miracles*, *Esoteric Healing*, *The Secret Doctrine*, *Urantia*, *The Secret Teachings of All*

Ages … I found the old "New Thought" writers like Neville Goddard, Wallace D. Wattles, Napoleon Hill and Norman Vincent Peale were all about the *power of belief.* Newer New Thought writers like Terrence McKenna, Rupert Sheldrake, and Alan Watts supported this concept.

Current New Science writers are now adding the often missed element of *emotions* to the science of manifestation and spontaneous healing - like Cynthia Sue Larson, Lynne McTaggart, Greg Braden, Bruce Lipton, and Joe Dispenza. Law of Attraction experts like Esther Hicks and Jean Slater, and gentle sages like Anita Moorjani, Wayne Dyer and Deepak Chopra all seem to be focusing on healing our lives and our world through intention powered by loving, generous, and grateful *feelings*. And my 10-year study and practice of Ho 'Oponopono has brought me more peace and joy through reconciliation than can be expressed here.

But it was my sister, Leslie, who brought me the most amazing story of manifestation not confined to the pages of a book! She told me the most amazing true story in late 1990, while I was working in news at the Chicago National Public Radio affiliate station. She told me about a woman she met in her writers group who, like many new, unpublished writers, was struggling to find time to write while making ends meet. She told Leslie it was her intention to live rent-free in luxury, so she could write her book without worrying about making rent money. She wrote this intention down on paper first thing upon waking up, and last thing before falling asleep, dated and signed it like a contract, for 40 days and 40 nights (a practice spread by word of mouth which I continued until now) ... and it worked!

She bumped into an older woman in the vegetable isle of a grocery store who casually asked her what she did for a living. She explained her ultimate goal and her financial challenges, and the woman answered her by inviting her to live temporarily in her mansion, where she could write her book rent-free (in complete luxury) - in exchange for house-sitting while she and her husband were away. My sister knew this woman, so it wasn't some exaggerated tale. The only caveat was she had to write two contracts with herself daily for the intended manifestations, and if she missed one - she had to start over from the beginning. Not great if you happen to miss a morning or an evening contract on the 30th day!

I immediately took pen to paper, but I decided to employ the other useful manifestation techniques I picked up along the way, like writing it in the present tense as if it has already happened. "I make $X amount of money a month", instead of "I will make $X amount ....."; "I am working at (fill in the blank)" instead of " I will find a job doing (fill in the blank)". Active verbs instead of passive, hopeful, future ones. I then added a big dose of gratitude at the end like, "Thank you, I love You" (Ho 'Oponopono), "Eternally Grateful", "With Love Always" … signed it and dated it like a contract between me and my higher self, the creative universe, God - or possibly all three!

BUT (and here is a big but) I found being young and busy I didn't always feel like writing it exactly the same time, the same way, the same length, with the same words … nor did I feel like writing it twice a day.

Now here is an important disclaimer: Very few things work for everyone all the time. So if you find something that works for you *most* of the time – consider it a win! So I decided to test out a modified version that worked much better for me which I share here:

1. I write my Manifestation Contract once a day – morning or night. Technically I was still writing it for "40 Days & 40 Nights".

2. I write it in the present tense only.

3. I write the same intentions differently each day to keep the creativity flowing and avoid boredom burnout.

4. If I miss a day/night I simply write it twice the next day ….

5. So, at the end of *40 Days & 40 Nights*, I have 40 signed and dated contracts with my intended manifestations full of love and gratitude as if I have already achieved them … and

6. it works beautifully!

In 1990, I intended for a bigger apartment, a piano, and a specific higher annual income that would allow for more travel. Having grown up in Trinidad and Egypt with my father Tom, and the Chicago suburbs with my mother, Patricia, I missed spending time in distant lands and cultures.

When I started writing my first contracts, I lived in a Chicago North-side studio apartment with a view of lake Michigan. I completed my *40 Days & 40 Nights* my way by January 1991, and within one month my neighbor across the hall had bought a large keyboard that looked like an upright piano.

He had an older keyboard looking for a new home. Without knowing if I was musical or not, Jim knocked on my door and offered me his old keyboard - which I gratefully accepted. Check box 1: manifestation intention "I have a piano (close enough!)".

Within two months, a one bedroom apartment opened up unexpectedly across the courtyard from me. After six years in my high-ceiling, spacious, bright, 1920s studio apartment ... I hired movers in February 1991 to help me move down three flights of stairs, across a snow-filled courtyard, and up three flights of stairs. Halfway through the job two burly men quit on me saying I could keep my money – too many stairs! Half of my furniture was still in the snowy courtyard. I called another mover and he came and completed the job alone! He carried all the furnishings and I carried all the boxes. It felt like a miracle we had both made it through this move. Check box 2: manifestation intention "I live in more space!"

Within three months, I was offered a position in news programming in Cologne, Germany for the national broadcasting network Radio Deutsche Welle to cover Eastern and Western European news in light of the Berlin Wall coming down. (I actually chipped away at it with my father until I realized it was full of asbestos.) Check box 3: manifestation intention "I earn $X annually so I can travel." That was what my father Tom would call a 'two-for': more money with travel in one go!

Within five months, my bags were packed and my mother Patricia took me to the airport the day before my 30th birthday, wishing me well on my new adventure. I said I would be back in about three years – that should be long enough to cure my travel-bug, but she shook her head saying no, it will be much longer than that. Though I called her weekly and came back to see her often, as she predicted, I did not return to live in the United States again until 2012 – some 21 years later!

After working for many European and American networks while living in Germany, England, Czechoslovakia and Romania, I left media to back-pack through Asia for a year with my British partner and twin flame John. We eloped in a town called Toya Bungkah (Holy Waters) in a Bali Aga ceremony provided by the villagers under the active volcano Mount Batur (that erupted two weeks after we climbed it and had our wedding ceremony at its foot).

A few years before meeting my husband, I had written in a *40 Days and 40 Nights* journal, "I live with a wonderful, loving, creative man, and a dog in the snow-capped mountains". After trekking Southeast Asia, some Pacific Islands, Australia and New Zealand for a year - we did just that for a few years in the Glenwood Springs canyon of Colorado, before returning to England for medical and health insurance reasons.

It was over a decade later before I felt the need to employ *40 Days & 40 Nights* again. We were still living in England and my husband was experiencing physical disabilities. I needed an income to support us while being his full-time caregiver, and while raising our toddler, Emily. With the successful opening of our organic nursery school Hedgehog Hill, and an amazing manager, Kim and staff, it became possible for me to do all of these full-time jobs at once. Again, my written signed contracts of heartfelt intentions during *40 Days & 40 Nights* had succeeded in providing exactly what I needed.

John passed into the next stage of his enlightened sojourn in 2006, but a course of *40/40* contracts signed shortly after his passing seemed *not* to have worked for me. I wrote, "I am a successful, best-selling author, with plenty of time and money to travel the world comfortably and safely." I was still studying metaphysics and quantum physics, but I just couldn't bring myself to write, as I had so gratefully intended ... until now 13 years later (from 2006 to 2019) - another 4!

Could it be that it *was* successful, but it took years instead of months to complete the manifestation process this time?

In 2019, four metaphysical YouTube Content Creators, Paulo (Spiritwalker channel), Shane (Unbiased & On the Fence channel), Vannessa (Vannessa VA channel) and myself (One Eileen Colts channel) published our first book, *Mandela Effect:*

Friend or Foe? exploring all aspects of the mysterious Mandela Effect phenomenon. (4) Now, this *40 Days & 40 Nights Manifestation Key* has decided to bring itself out through me - the very same year. Another 'two-for' Dad!

Conclusion: my perceived failed *40 Days & 40 Nights* exercise in 2006 was delayed, but finally succeeded in 2019 - 13 years later. Now I agree that 13 Earth years may seem like a long time for manifesting something specific in an Earth lifetime but – not so long in the duration of the universe in which it is occurring!

Please note that I have found manifestation fairly easy most of my life, because I truly believe with all my heart that 1. it is possible and 2. that I deserve it. This makes me feel excited with anticipation and joyful that life is so magical. Results may vary depending on how you feel about these two essential manifestation elements concerning yourself and the world. BIG hint here – believe it and know you deserve it as you are writing it!

CHAPTER 4
Forming New Habits & Beliefs

There once was a plastic surgeon named Doctor Maxwell Maltz, who discovered that if he changed a patient's face in some significant way, it took them on average about 21 days to get used to seeing their new face, and accepting it as normal. When patients had an arm or a leg amputated, he noticed the patients would sense their phantom limbs for about 21 days too. In 1960, Dr. Maltz published his book *Psycho-Cybernetics*, which became a bestseller. (5)

This established the idea that it takes repeating something for at least 21 days to establish it as a new habit or belief. And conversely, it takes a minimum of about 21 days for an old belief or habit to be erased. In other words, if you see something often enough you accept it as fact. This pertains to thoughts as well. If you think something often enough it becomes factual for you.

In Law of Attraction lore and practice, we have come to understand that everything starts as a thought. If you think something often enough it becomes a belief. And if you add your emotions to you thoughts and beliefs and take action upon them – manifestation quickens. Much more than if you simply repetitively only *think* about what you wish to manifest. Feeling, gratitude, and action are key to realizing your dreams in a material matrix.

If you apply this theory to practicing something

repetitively for *40 Days & 40 Nights*, you can see that is ample time to dissolve old paradigms and establish new ones that better serve you, your family, community, world, universe ....

It seems quantum science is showing repeatedly how thoughts and feelings influence and change matter. Look up the Observer Effect. If your thoughts and feelings will change your material world willy nilly, then why not harness that power for better control of what you create and attract? Psychology supports this. People with an 'external locus of control' tend to view the world around them more negatively. They feel they are the victim of other people and circumstances. The negative outlook results in negative feelings and actions that attract more negative people and situations to them, creating a feedback loop for more negative feelings. The opposite is true, with people who have an 'internal locus of control' tending to feel more in control of their experiences and environment, and as such, attracting more positive people and situations, creating the biofeedback loop that encourages more positive beliefs – feeling – action - experience – beliefs – feeling – action and so on.

In terms of controlling feelings in order to make them less reactionary and more appropriate, that momentary pause, or breath before reaction is often all it takes for more reasonable emotions to prevail.

So, the question we may never answer emphatically is: *Does 40 Days & 40 Nights* (as a metaphysical manifestation tool) work because it employs repetitive behavior and belief for more than the duration of time needed to establish new beliefs and habits - replacing ineffective beliefs and habits in the process? Or does it work because 40 is a sacred and magical (of the Magi) number for **miraculous manifestation?** Is there any way to prove it one way or the other, and is there any need to do so - if it is a combination of both?!

Your thoughts rule your beliefs. Your beliefs create your feelings. Your combined thoughts, beliefs and feelings dictate your actions. Your thoughts, beliefs, feelings and actions create not only your world, but our shared collective world. You affect me and I affect you and the seven billion others ... see how important your positivity is to Earth and us in the here and now? Because only what is within (spirit) - is reflected without (matter). See **Hermetic Laws**.

In summary I completely trust that:

THOUGHTS ARE THINGS WITH WINGS AND OUR FEELINGS GIVE THEM FLIGHT.

YOUR THOUGHTS WILL RETURN TO YOU IN THE FORM OF MATERIAL EXPERIENCES - IF YOU FEED THEM ENOUGH OF YOUR EMOTIONS.

WARNING: THIS IS TRUE FOR POSITIVE, NEUTRAL AND NEGATIVE THOUGHTS.

Many believe the reality matrix around us on the outside is a reflection of how we feel about ourselves and our world on the inside. As well as how the entire species thinks, feels and acts. So our repeated thoughts become our beliefs, which produce our feelings, which direct our physical actions in matter collectively too.

Repeated Thoughts = Beliefs = Feelings = Actions. (On the individual and collective levels.)

Think of feelings (emotions) as supercharged thoughts which have a profound effect on matter. Many of us believe thoughts from the brain are more electric in nature because of the electrical firing between synapses; and feelings from the heart are more magnetic in nature due to the pumping action of the heart; while actions are kinetic in nature. Though there are many states and levels of energy - these three combined forces create and edit the matter around us constantly. Kind of like your lungs breathe and your heart beats without you telling them to. Manifesting matter around you as a direct result of your feelings is an autonomic action. Time to make it deliberate. Time to stop manifesting on accident and manifest on purpose by directing and orchestrating your feelings towards desired results!

The early New Thought movement focused on controlling thoughts alone with books by Napoleon Hill, Wallace Wattles and Norman Vincent Peale. However, it took another century for us to understand our thoughts are only the beginning of matrix management – feelings are necessary to give our thoughts enough oomph to manifest, and action speeds the whole process up. That is why just thinking something over and over does not manifest desires very well, even after they have become firm beliefs. Feelings help speed up manifestation by giving them the magnetic heart energy to draw them to you quicker than electric thoughts alone. But when you add thoughts, feelings and actions in a focused way to manifest a specific goal or desire - this trinity or trifecta of energies produces faster manifestation in a material world by pulling the intention out of the 'ethers of possibility' into the physical world of matter. This is especially true if you add a fourth force: the spoken word (more on this later).

THOUGHT + FEELING + SPOKEN WORD + ACTION ARE THE FOUR PILLARS OF THIS BOOK.

This works for the collective in jointly creating, editing, and maintaining the material world through collectively held beliefs and feelings too. We can call this **Matrix Management**. Look up the Mandela Effect; (read my other book *Mandela Effect Friend or Foe?*; and take a page out of any of Eckhart Tolle's books and videos to be present in the *now* – which is the only place where the power to create or change everything resides! And pause before reacting to anything to consider how you would like to respond. Respond don't React.

This is important for us/we as well. If the collective group is feeling scared, angry and insecure, it might be willing to part with more of its hard-earned money in the form of taxes to build more bombs and walls. So it behooves the weapons manufacturers to keep the collective in a constant state of fear. That is a very profitable emotion for a few, but not so profitable for the many. This also applies to diseases and pharmaceuticals, and anything where manipulated group emotion results in some form of control or profitability for a smaller group of humans. They know and we know this is coming to a natural evolutionary end as the Sleeping Giant (humanity or the "Sheeple" but I prefer "Sleeple") awakens to emotional manipulation used to manage the material matrix to favor the few over the many. Now we step into our personal individual power in order to empower the collective - as co-creators here like never before!

Fear is a perfect state for manifesting negative outcomes and experiences. Love, joy, peace are perfect states for manifesting positive outcomes and experiences. Believe it or not, your emotions are under only your control. It is not what *happens* to you that matters, as much as how you *react* to what happens to you - that matters most. This is why no one can make you feel anything ever. They may do or say what they wish, but it is entirely up to you how you respond to what they do or say. (Respond don't React.)

We exist moment by moment by moment by moment … we do not actually exist in the past or in the future at any point in our entire life in the here-now. In this way, life in matter is a perennial now with the illusion or memory of a past, and the hopes and dreams of a future. This explains why all time is happening at once - because you only ever have a long string of nows in which to exist, move, change, fear, love, act, and be. Focusing on the past can result in feelings of regret, while dwelling on the future may produce feelings of uncertainty. Dwelling on the present is called **mindfulness** and is where you exercise your true power to manifest within this spirit-body-matrix.

Power to react appropriately, power to make changes, power to influence the whole, power to steer your life ... is only ever exercised in the moment. Your life can be measured in your responses moment by moment over a lifetime, because when you are looking back - that is all you have, and there is your power. Those who study avatars know that miracles come from *states of being* and not from mere wishes, thoughts, beliefs, feelings or even actions.

The Buddhic or "middle way" (sometimes called the Narrow Path), is to look at everything and if it is positive appreciate it, if it is negative transmute it through forgiveness, and if it is neither negative nor positive then remain neutral. This is controlling your state of being, which controls your manifest world.

THERE IS NO SUCH THING AS NEW AGE OR ANCIENT WISDOM. THERE ARE ONLY YOUR THOUGHTS AND THEY ARE BOTH WISE AND MUNDANE.

To manifest more consistently it is wise to learn how to control negative thoughts before they turn into negative words and negative actions attracting negative relationships and negative experiences (Law of Attraction – as like attracts like).

It is not as difficult as it seems:

1. Notice the negative thought.

2. Stop thinking it.

3. Say to yourself or out loud: I choose to think positive thoughts right now.

4. Think or say out loud the exact opposite of the negative topic in a positive way.

5. That is it. Move on with your day.

Never criticize your negative thoughts, as this only grows more negativity. Remember positive people tend to draw more positive people and events to them, while the opposite is true. And it is never too late to become more mindfully aware of your thoughts to increase their positivity. Eventually positive thoughts will come to you more often naturally - if you continue to replace any negative ones with positive ones immediately.

Candice Pert's book, *Molecules of Emotions*, shows how feelings change the chemistry in our bodies. (6) This means feelings can alter matter of the body and can be harnessed to heal. Why live negatively when you can flood your body and our shared matrix with love - of which gratitude and forgiveness are but expressions?

For quicker manifestation, I have learned it's not only important to *feel* your intentions, but to imagine already having *achieved* them with all your senses and to *act* upon them. However, in order for this to work, it is crucial to practice the **no-harm principle** for manifesting anything!

IF IT HARMS ANYONE OR ANYTHING, THEN IT IS NOT GOOD. IF IT IS NOT GOOD FOR EVERYONE AND EVERYTHING CONCERNED, THEN IT IS NOT GOOD FOR YOU. SIMPLE LAW OF MANIFESTATION!

Not coincidentally, manifestations work more quickly the more they benefit others.

Gratitude is very powerful fuel for manifesting. It has been determined by some that well-being and balance is the intrinsic nature of the universe we find ourselves in. This explains why we crave peace, harmony and ease so much in work, home, relationships – life! Gratitude for what you have and gratitude for what is coming is so important to speeding up and maintaining the manifestation process as your *natural* state of being.

Matrix Management is in *all* of our minds, hearts, and hands - not just the few who manipulate the many. This is why they even bother to manipulate the many, which takes a great deal of time, money, and effort on their part. If you want to start creating your reality instead of their reality – you can start doing this with your own *40 Days & 40 Nights Manifestation Key* practice and exercise.

CHAPTER 5

Let's Get Started

The best time to start *40 Days & 40 Nights* is right now. You can buy a beautiful dedicated journal for it, or an inexpensive school notebook works just as well. Place the pen and notebook next to your bed and either first thing in the morning after waking, or last thing at night before sleeping:

Write down one or more desires you would like to manifest in your life. These can include making more money, finding a partner, improving a relationship, getting a promotion, finding a new job, changing fields entirely, improving certain skills, seeing more of the world, having more time with family, losing weight, gaining weight, healing your mind, healing your emotions, increasing spiritual skills ... there are no limits so long as it pertains to YOU!

This is not an exercise to help or change others so much as it is an exercise to attract into your life what you clearly desire - unless you directly care for them, as in elderly parents, children and pets. You may utilize *40 Days & 40 Nights* for yourself and anyone in your direct care. Prayers are better for helping others you are not directly responsible for.

Because we largely get what we ask for - it is important to be clear and specific when writing your desired manifestations in your *40 days & 40 Nights* notebook or journal. Instead of asking to make more money state, "I earn x amount per month or year." State your desires as if you have already achieved them. Instead of, " I will earn x per month." Write "I earn x per month."

You may write your intentions in detailed long-hand, or short lists. In fact, change it up from time to time. Use numbers and bullet points, or use paragraphs. The more creative you make this, the quicker it will go for you, and the more fun you will have while doing it.

How many intentions should you include? That is up to you, but fewer seems better in terms of quick effective manifestation. Plus it will become a chore if you have to write dozens of intentions down on paper every day or night. Keep it short and simple, and specific.

Use feelings and all five (or six) senses to give your intentions umph! Feel them, see them, hear them, use all your senses to imagine what it feels like to have them right now.

End your daily manifestation contract with gratitude and love. Before you sign it add, "with loving gratitude now and forever" or something along those lines.

Then sign it any way you please. Some days I sign my full name, some nights I just sign my first name – whatever feels right in the moment.

Date it at the top or bottom like a formal contract.

Write your intentions contract at least once a day

or night, but don't panic if you miss one. Just write two the next day. So long as you have 40 signed, detailed, specific, present-tense statements of desired manifestations, dated and signed, with gratitude, at the end of *40 days and 40 nights* – it is *almost* done.

Now speak them out loud and add some action, small or great, to help your desires break through from the 'quantum field of possibility' – into your physical reality. If you want a specific car – go test drive it. A house – look at houses for sale in your area. A relationship – sign-up for activities where like-minded people go. A new job that better suits your gifts – search online for jobs and apply. Even if you don't have the skills required sometimes passion for the job carries the day.

40 Days & 40 Nights Steps:

- Get a dedicated journal or notebook, and pen.

- Place them by your bed.

- Write your intended manifestations every morning or night; or both.

- Write one or more intentions.

- Be specific and use details.

- Write them in the present tense as if they are already yours, or have already occurred.

- Write intentions in paragraphs, or use bullet point lists.

- Really feel what you are writing about.

- Visualize them with all senses.

- Close with gratitude and pause to really feel it as you give thanks.

- Check they do not cause harm to anyone or anything.

- Sign it and date it like a contract.

- Speak the intentions and gratitude out loud.

- Act on them is some way daily.

- Allow them to occur in their own way without worry or doubt (more on this later).

- Now - it is done!

An important question is how long will it take for my manifestations to materialize? As you have seen from my personal experiences with it - it can take days, months, years or even decades. This is dependent on many individual and personal factors.

But the more you practice manifestation, the more natural it becomes, and the quicker it succeeds. Like all skills practice makes perfect. And if something doesn't manifest for you quickly enough - ask yourself if there are any good reasons why?

Intentions should serve your higher purpose, and should not violate the free will of another and their higher purpose. In other words, if you are asking that a specific person fall deeply and madly in love with you – that may not serve your purpose in life or theirs. It is more than wise to keep intentions practical and purposeful to aid you and others in some way. Hint: this last statement is an important key to manifestation success.

CHAPTER 6

Sample Writing

January 1, 2020

I Samantha Smith am eternally grateful for

- Earning $70,000 per year starting now

- In graphic design using my talents and gifts

- With my talented smart generous kind

  loving partner

- And for my fully-healed strong ankle!

  With my love always,

  Sam

  xo

January 2, 2020

I am so happy for receiving my raise at work to seventy-thousand dollars a year starting this year! I have successfully changed careers, using my natural talents and skills in graphic design. I have found a wonderful mate who is romantic, generous, creative and kind. My ankle is now completely healed and stronger than ever before!

Thank you so very much!

I Love you,

Samantha S. Smith

Dear God,

I am so grateful for my raise at work for seventy-thousand dollars a year and being promoted to the graphic design department, where I use my talents more creatively! I also so appreciate getting along with everyone - especially my boss, who has much appreciation for me and my work!

I am so very lucky to have found my amazing partner who appreciates me. He/she is smart, creative, fun, loyal, generous, very kind and loving. We enjoy spending time and traveling together, and deeply love each other.

I am so happy my ankle is now completely healed, flexible and stronger than ever. I walk long distances and even run now!

I am eternally grateful for these and all I receive in health and abundance now and forever!

With My Love Always!

Sam Smith

1/3/2020

(You may add smiley faces, hearts, drawings of your manifest intentions Xs and Os …. throughout.)

Do you see how all of these samples cover specific details on the same intentions, but are written in different ways in order to maintain interest and creativity? If you prefer to write identical statements every day or night – that works too and ensures you never leave anything out.

CHAPTER 7

Refining Your Desires

Think about the one to three most important goals you would like to achieve as soon as possible. Make sure they are important to you, or put them off to a future *40 Days & 40 Nights* exercise.

Chances are they require an increase in two important things: money and time. Instead of simply writing down you want more money now and how much and how you will receive it – why not leave that part up to the creative universe or God to figure out? What you really desire is what the increased money can buy you: a house, a new house, a bigger house ... a car, a new car, a more expensive car ... travel to see loved ones, travel to see the world ... university courses .... Think of the specific things you would like to have, and more importantly, think about the specific things you would like to do. Specific, important, experiences you would like to have that increased money or increased free time could bring you, and ask for those in a positive, grateful way in the present tense – as if you already have them. At the end of the day, experiences are what we came here for, and are far more important than getting more stuff. You take your experiences into the hereafter and they determine your next ones. Try doing that with a mansion, a boat, a diamond ring ….

To take it to the next level, try replacing: "I make more money or x amount."

With: "I always have more money than I need to pay all of my bills easily and on time, and to do (fill in the blank)!"

Or, "I make plenty of money to pay all of my bills easily and to experience (what?)!"

… to visit loved ones, to travel to (where), to help a loved one buy their first home, to take university courses, to study piano, art, music, dance, to work with children, animals, to help others in (this) specific way ….

Or combine them: " I am so grateful I have more money than I need right now and always to purchase a new 2400 square foot house and to travel to Africa in comfort and safety."

When it comes to creating specific relationships, be specific about the character traits your desired partner will have that are most important to you.

"I am so grateful for having met my loving, loyal, creative, kind, generous and successful partner (man, woman, husband, wife) right now!"

"I am completely open to meeting my soulmate today."

Be specific about improved health and healing requests for yourself and those you directly care for. "I am blessed to have flexible, strong joints that move easily and freely now and always" (healing arthritis).

"I am so very grateful my child (name) breathes easily and freely now and in all ways forever!" (healing asthma).

"We are celebrating my father (name) successful hip replacement surgery and full recovery in March!"

Use active expressive words: I am grateful, I appreciate, Thank you for, I am blessed with, I have, I found, I am, We have, We love, We appreciate, I travel, I earn, I do, now, always, forever, in all directions of time, with ease, peace, relief, comfort, growth, healing, health, plenty, bountiful, more than we need …. Notice the lack of negative words and phrases like, pain-free, disease, poverty, debt, lack …. In programming the subconscious mind double negatives Do Not make a positive, like:

- "I don't feel any more pain" becomes "My body is completely at ease and only feels positive healthy sensations".

- "I am not sad anymore" becomes "I am happy now and forever".

- "I am no longer broke" becomes "I pay all of my bills easily now and forever and have spare cash to do x".

Charge up your intentions with creative, active words and visualize yourself doing your intentions with all of your senses while you are writing them in your notebook.

After you have written them down for the day/night, and you have signed and dated the contract, give gratitude for them, visualize them, speak them out loud; and as soon as possible take action on them, great or small, to demonstrate to yourself and the universe that you really do want them now. Even symbolic actions help.

What one to three physical things, specific experiences, improved health, healings, new or improved relationships do you want to achieve most of all right now? Start with those.

Though you can do the *40 Days & 40 Nights* exercise as often as you like, it is important to take reasonable breaks in between in order to keep it fresh. Anything, no matter how fun or exciting, quickly becomes repetitive, boring and a chore if done too much or too often.

CHAPTER 8

Ask, Command, then Allow

If you have had the opportunity to study some energetic healing modalities, you may have already learned the **spoken word** is extremely powerful. So, this is an additional manifestation key to be practiced with your *40 Days & 40 Nights Manifestation Key* of written, signed contracts for improved manifestation.

Now would be a good time to point out that even without directed empowered intention you are manifesting here in a material matrix constantly - with every thought, word, feeling, decision, action you make. The difference lies in manifesting *without purpose* versus manifesting *with purpose*; manifesting *slowly* versus manifesting *quicker*; and manifesting *anything* versus manifesting what *you* desire.

Ask God or source energy out loud for what you would like to see, do, have or experience here in matter now. You do not command God or source energy, that would be considered overly demanding and rude. However, only a few here know that they have been put here by God, source energy, the creative universe to lovingly do exactly that with all lower energy including matter. You are here to **command matter** – this is your manifest destiny and responsibility! You may not be able to command God or source energy, but the physical world of matter is your playground to command, shape, build, create, edit, erase, start over ... as you please, so long as it does not harm anyone or anything (including violating someone's free will). And God put you here to do this! If God did not put you here to do this – then how are you here shaping and experiencing matter? Perhaps to learn more about your true nature in order to level up into a more individually responsible matrix management role.

ASK GOD, BUT COMMAND MATTER IN A WAY THAT BENEFITS ALL, THEN ACT + ALLOW MIRACLES TO MANIFEST!

The biggest mistake new purposeful-manifesters make is to ask God and then *ask* matter to manifest *for* them. That is a bit weaselly, indicates you a weak passive player in the process, and though it can eventually work, it can take much longer.

The other mistake is to ask and then worry about it: if, how, when, and where it will become manifest.

I find it helps to ask God, source energy, or the creative universe in writing and out loud for what you desire most here-now that in no way harms another and is for the best possible outcome for all concerned. This covers all the bases for speedy manifestation. And if you can do this in groups of like-minded people at the same time – watch miracles manifest instantaneously! (See Lynne McTaggart's *Power of Eight* book.) (8)

Thank God, source energy, or the creative

universe for hearing and answering your request.

Then *command matter to move for you in a way

that will produce your manifestation request as

quickly as possible. Finally, act on it often and then

allow it to be-come (come+be) in its own way and

time.

Worrying about *if* your manifestation will occur

is doubting the power of God or source energy.

Dictating *how* God or source energy answers your

request slows it down, because God or source

energy is so creative they may bring it to you in an

entirely unexpected but faster way. Dictating in

* "Truly I tell you, if you have faith as small as a mustard seed,
you can say to this mountain, 'Move from here to there,' and it
will move." - Matthew 17:20

your intentions how it comes to you - may slow it down, but add it if the how is as important to you as the end result.

Often called the **Art of Allowing**, this is the letting go of all worry, doubt and expectation - trusting fully that God heard you and will answer your request for manifestation help in God's way. *Ask and you shall receive* is stated clearly in the Bible, many religious writings, and all Law of Attraction guidelines. Feeling it, giving gratitude for it, speaking it out loud and acting on it are equally important, but by far the most challenging part seems to be the letting go and allowing it to *become* in its own magical way and time.

Three more important resources to boost your daily, natural, creative manifestation skills may be found in the books, cds and videos by: Cynthia Sue Larson, like her book *Quantum Jumps* (8); Anita Moorjani, like her book *Dying To Be Me* (9); and Esther and Jerry Hicks, like their *Getting into the Vortex* book/cd (10).

CHAPTER 9

And So It Is Done

Now you understand the power of adding emotions, gratitude, action and allowance to your intended manifestations – what about the **spoken word**?

Perhaps the biggest expert source on The Word is the Bible: "In the beginning was the Word, and the Word was with God, and the Word was God."

John 1:1

Jesus answered, "It is written: 'Man shall not live on bread alone, but on every word that comes from the mouth of God.'"

Matthew 4:4

"Do not merely listen to the word, and so deceive yourselves. Do what it says."

James 1:22

"For the word of God is alive and active, sharper than any double-edged sword, it penetrates even to dividing soul and spirit, joints and marrow, it judges the thoughts and attitudes of the heart."

Hebrews 4:12

"The grass withers and the flowers fall, but the word of our God endures forever."

Isaiah 40:8

"He humbled you, causing you to hunger and then feeding you with manna, which neither you nor your ancestors had known, to teach you that man does not live on bread alone but on every word

that comes from the mouth of the Lord."

Deuteronomy 8:3

"Heaven and earth will pass away, but my words

will never pass away."

Matthew 24:35

"The unfolding of your words gives light;

it gives understanding to the simple."

Psalm 119:130

"The Word became flesh and made his dwelling

among us. We have seen his glory, the glory of the

one and only Son, who came from the Father, full of

grace and truth."

John 1:14

"All Scripture is God-breathed and is useful for

teaching, rebuking, correcting and training in righteousness, so that the servant of God may be thoroughly equipped for every good work."

Timothy 3:16-17

The Word in Islam

Muslims believe the Quran contains the literal words of God, which were spoken in Arabic. The Word Allah means "God" in Islam. The word is thought to be derived by contraction from al-ilāh, which means "the god", and is related to El and Elah - the Hebrew and Aramaic words for God which became Elohim.

Words are powerful creators in energy, hence the word **spell**-ing as in the magic ordering of words (used by Magi - magicians). Which is why words created and used by ruling religious, financial, governing authorities often have double meanings like "blessed" for some means b-less than I; citizenship means of the citi on my ship in maritime law (which implies owner-ship and is why you must have a birth certificate (as they berth boats at their docs with documents) .... There is an exhaustive list of the true, secret, ruling, magi and sigil meanings of words and symbols used to maintain order to benefit the few over the many here now, but that requires your own research. Know it is not necessary to understand them to overcome them by increasing your own personal power of manifestation. Focus on the positive (you) instead of the negative (them) to improve your life and the whole shared *here-now*!

They can simply join in or fall away when enough are practicing their personal power of manifestation.

Words have always been considered powerful. Not only for simple communication. Words encourage, uplift, inspire and heal. They express love and create songs when merged with music. Poetry reflects their art, but they can also cruelly tear people down and incite fear, hate, even murder and war. So use your words wisely and set them lovingly free to empower, protect, and uplift yourself and others!

Thoughts are usually populated with internal words spoken by your internal voice and those words belong to you. Remember:

THOUGHTS ARE THINGS WITH WINGS –
THEY HAVE A WAY OF RETURNING TO YOU.

REPEATED THOUGHTS DICTATE BELIEFS, SO
CHOOSE YOUR MEDIA WISELY.

FEELINGS AND ACTIONS FUEL YOUR BELIEFS
INTO MATERIAL MANIFESTATION.

BUT IT ALL STARTS WITH
THREE SIMPLE WORDS:
GOD, LOVE, AND YOU.

ABOUT THE AUTHOR

EILEEN COLTS

Eileen grew up in the suburbs of Chicago, Cairo and the coconut jungles of Trinidad & Tobago. She opened the first expatriate nursery school in Maadi, Egypt in 1979, and then completed her B.A. magna cum laude from Loyola University, Chicago with a major in journalism and minor in (child) psychology, 1985.

Fortunate to land her first post-university job at the Chicago NPR affiliate radio station, she started as a producer/reporter in children's programming, but left as the morning news anchor and City Hall reporter for a European network posting five years later.

Eileen initially joined the German national broadcasting network Radio Deutsche Welle as a news editor, reporter, director and host for their international English Service, but left to freelance report Eastern European news, based in Cologne, Prague and Bucharest, for National Public Radio (NPR), Associated Press (AP), Pacifica Radio, Canadian Broadcasting Corporation (CBC), Radio France, and Vatican Radio.

In London, Eileen worked as a media consultant for international corporations and energy companies, before starting a family with her husband John, and settling down to open one of the country's first organic nursery schools. She became a healthy childcare writer, speaker and advocate (published under her maiden name Eileen McIntyre).

Though her professional life primarily involved children and media, her private passion focused on world religions and quantum physics. Looking for God and the meaning of life, she was certain it would cross the boundaries of the mystical and the scientific, so her studies involved science, philosophy, metaphysics, religion and mythology.

She credits her NDE in Egypt in 1977 following an immunization anaphylaxis for leading her into the mystic's private life, after remaining fully conscious and watching a medical team resuscitate her lifeless body.

Eileen returned to the United States in 2012, where the Mandela Effect soon caught her attention. She found likeminded people on YouTube putting a name to something she has experienced since 1995, and recalls her mother experiencing since the 1970s. She began her YouTube channel One (Eileen Colts) in 2016 on the advice of Shane to share Mandela Effect experiences and observations, but soon moved into the spiritual and metaphysical realms of quantum mysticism and contact disclosure.

In her book, *Mandela Effect: Friend or Foe?* with fellow YouTube channel metaphysical researchers Paulo Pinto (Spiritwalker), Shane Robinson (Unbiased & On the Fence) and Vanessa VA channel, Eileen concludes the Mandela Effect is a Quantum Awakening of humanity. "The New Human will easily understand this phenomenon and so much more. This is the beginning of a major evolutionary change. Consider it a marker or a signpost for generations to come. When did people first start to see how their collective thoughts manage matter collectively? When they started seeing the Mandela Effect."

Eileen is a contributing recipient of a Corporation for Public Broadcast (CPB) Award 1989 for Live Concert Production (Director); and a National Education Association (NEA) Award 1986 for Excellence in Children's Programming (Producer/Host).

END NOTES:

1. The Electronic Text Corpus of Sumerian Literature, Faculty of Oriental Studies, University of Oxford, http://etcsl.orinst.ox.ac.uk/, accessed 3.12.2019.

2. Sitchin, Zecharia. *The 12th Planet*: Book 1 of the Earth Chronicles. HarperCollins, 2007

3. News, October 4, 2017, "The Super-Earth that Came Home for Dinner", https://www.jpl.nasa.gov/news/news.php?feature=6964, accessed 12.04.19

4. Colts, Eileen; Pinto, Paulo M.; Robinson, Shane C; VA, Vanessa. *Mandela Effect: Friend or Foe?* 11:11 Publishing House, 2019.

5. Maltz, Maxwell. *Psycho-Cybernetics* the Letters of Sigmond Freud and Oskar Pfister. Simon and Schuster, 1960.

6. Pert, Candace B. Ph. D. *Molecules of Emotion*. Scribner, 1997.

7. McTaggart, Lynne. *The Power of Eight: the Miraculous Healing Power of Small Groups*. Atria Books, 2017.

8. Larson, Cynthia Sue. *Quantum Jumps: an Extraordinary Science of Happiness and Prosperity*. RealityShifters, 2013.

9. Moorjani, Anita. *Dying To Be Me*. Hay House, 2012.

10. Hicks, Esther, et al. *Getting into the Vortex: Guided Meditations CD and User Guide*. Hay House, 2011.

YOUR NOTES:

Made in the USA
Columbia, SC
05 October 2021